W9-CBQ-451

Manny Pacquiao

By Jon M. Fishman

Lerner Publications ◆ Minneapolis

Copyright © 2016 by Lerner Publishing Group, Inc.

All rights reserved. International copyright secured. No part of this book may be reproduced, stored in a retrieval system, or transmitted in any form or by any means—electronic, mechanical, photocopying, recording, or otherwise—without the prior written permission of Lerner Publishing Group, Inc., except for the inclusion of brief quotations in an acknowledged review.

Lerner Publications Company
A division of Lerner Publishing Group, Inc.
241 First Avenue North
Minneapolis, MN 55401 USA

For reading levels and more information, look up this title at www.lernerbooks.com.

Library of Congress Cataloging-in-Publication Data

Fishman, Jon M.
Manny Pacquiao / by Jon M. Fishman.
pages cm. — (Amazing athletes)
Includes bibliographical references and index.
ISBN 978-1-4677-9387-2 (lb : alk. paper) — ISBN 978-1-4677-9623-1 (pb : alk. paper) — ISBN 978-1-4677-9624-8 (eb pdf)
1. Pacquiao, Manny, 1978– 2. Boxers (Sports) —Philippines—Biography. I. Title.
GV1132.P25F57 2016
796.83092—dc23 [B] 2015027459

Manufactured in the United States of America
1 – BP – 12/31/15

TABLE OF CONTENTS

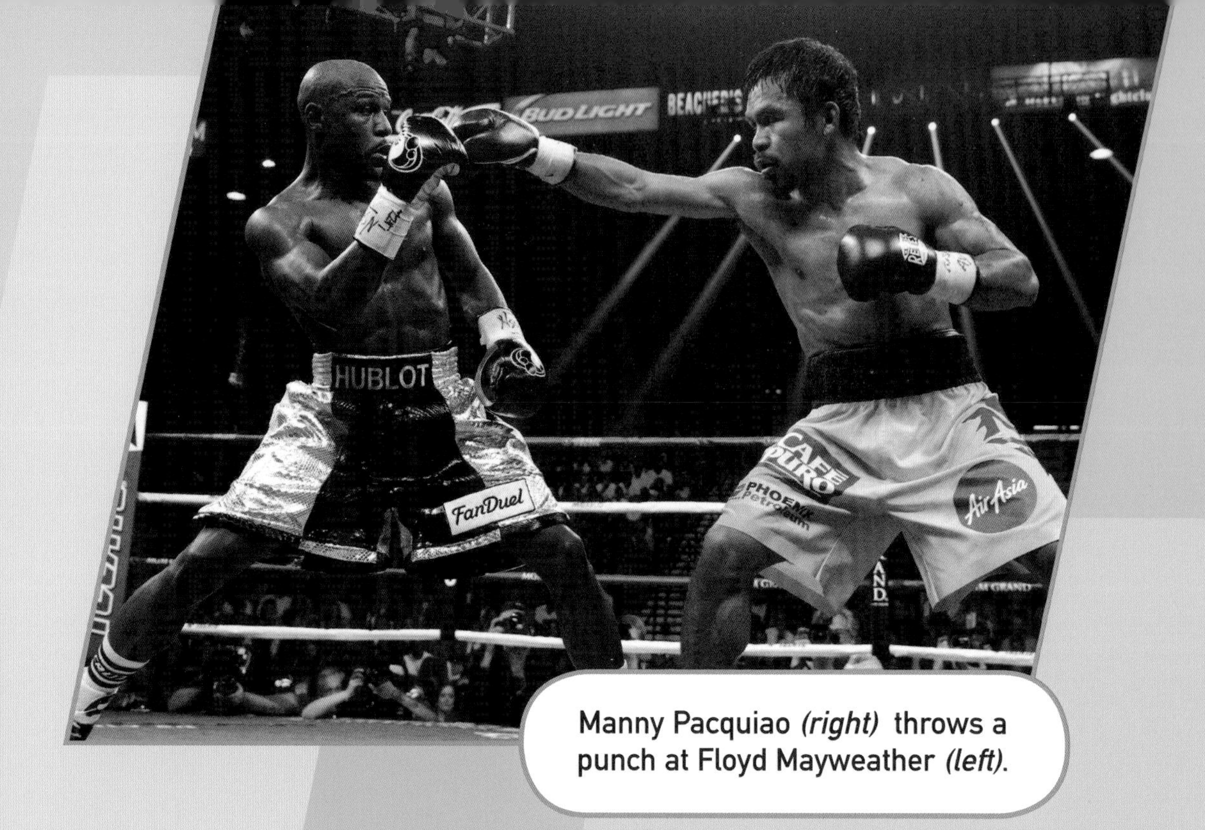

Manny Pacquiao *(right)* throws a punch at Floyd Mayweather *(left)*.

FIGHT OF THE CENTURY

Boxer Manny Pacquiao threw a powerful left-handed punch. It connected with the face of Floyd Mayweather. Manny attacked as Mayweather bounced into the ropes. Manny fired a burst of punches. The huge crowd clapped and cheered.

Manny was boxing Floyd Mayweather on May 3, 2015. The fight was at the MGM Grand Garden Arena in Las Vegas, Nevada. Many people called it the fight of the century. Mayweather had a perfect boxing record of 47 wins and 0 losses. Manny is one of the greatest boxing champions of all time. He has won world championships

Mayweather lunges at Manny.

across eight different weight classes. No other boxer has matched that feat.

More than 16,000 people watched the fight in Las Vegas. Many more watched on TV, especially in the Philippines. Manny was born in the Philippines. He is a huge star in his home country. "He represents the hopes of so many," said Manny's **trainer**, Freddie Roach.

Fans of Manny watch the fight between him and Mayweather on TV at a public plaza in the Philippines.

Manny chased Mayweather around the ring. Mayweather focused on defense. He didn't want to get caught by one of Manny's fierce punches.

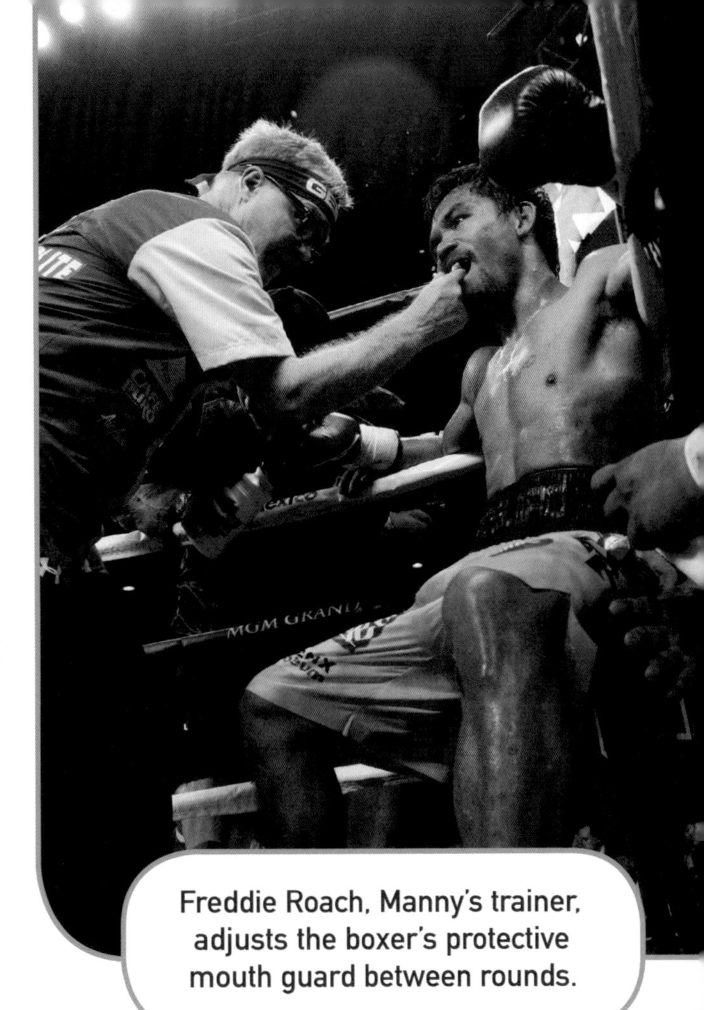

Freddie Roach, Manny's trainer, adjusts the boxer's protective mouth guard between rounds.

In the sixth round, Manny backed Mayweather against the ropes again. Manny let loose with **combinations**. He sent **jabs** and **hooks** toward Mayweather. Manny ducked and tried an **uppercut**. But Mayweather's defense was too good. Manny couldn't land a clean punch.

In the 12th and final round, the crowd chanted "Manny, Manny!" He fought harder than ever. But Mayweather stayed away from Manny's big punches. The result would come down to the judges' decision. A few minutes after the fight ended, the announcer told the crowd that Mayweather had won.

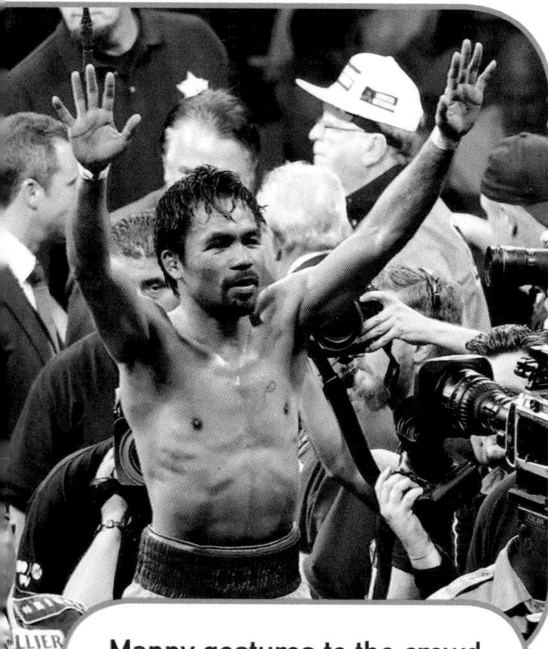
Manny gestures to the crowd after losing to Mayweather.

Manny and his fans were disappointed. "I thought I won the fight," he said. Manny took a vacation after the big event. But he'll be back in the ring soon. Losing to Mayweather won't keep the champion with the big smile down for long.

Manny became interested in boxing at a young age.

FISTS OF FURY

Emmanuel "Manny" Dapidran Pacquiao was born in Kibawe, Philippines, on December 17, 1978. The Philippines is a country in southeast Asia. More than 7,100 islands make up the nation. Kibawe is near the center of Mindanao, the second-largest island.

When Manny was a young boy, he and his family moved. They went south to the city of General Santos. They didn't have enough money for a home of their own. "We were poor, very poor," Manny later wrote. They lived with a close relative, Sardo Mejia.

Manny had a lot of energy. He loved the action of Bruce Lee movies. Lee starred in many **martial arts** films. Manny practiced his martial arts moves on a banana tree in his yard.

Bruce Lee *(above)* was one of Manny's idols.

When Manny was 12 years old, he dropped out of school. His family

Manny trained very hard.

needed money. The boy helped his family sell food on the street. He also began taking boxing lessons with Sardo Mejia. Manny wanted to be like Bruce Lee. But Manny didn't look tough enough to Mejia. "[Manny] was twelve and he had no muscle on him at all, and at first I couldn't see him being a fighter," Mejia said.

Manny and Mejia practiced boxing for months. Like his hero Bruce Lee, Manny moved like lightning. His punches were fast and strong. He seemed to fly around the ring on his quick feet. Mejia was soon convinced that Manny could be a world champion someday.

Manny began boxing in local **bouts**. If he won a fight, he would receive 100 pesos. That was about $3.50 in US dollars. He gave half the money to his family. Manny would often spend the rest on candy. Sometimes after winning a fight, Manny would climb a tree and throw treats down to his friends.

Manny loves to sing. He has released two music albums, *Laban Nating Lahat Ito* and *Pac-Man Punch*.

Manny trained at the LM Gym in Manila as a teenager.

BOXING DAYS

When Manny was about 15 years old, he got into an argument with his father. Manny ran away from home. He snuck onto a boat that was headed for Manila. The capital city of the Philippines is on the island of Luzon.

In January 1995, Manny had his first big boxing match in Manila. He beat Edmund Ignacio in four rounds. Manny kept fighting and won most of the time. Many of his matches were shown on a TV show called *Blow by Blow*. Filipino boxing fans fell in love with Manny's quick moves and wide smile.

Manny fought against Chatchai Sasakul *(above)* in Thailand.

Manny kept winning fights, and he kept moving up the boxing rankings. On December 4, 1998, he had the biggest fight of his life. Manny faced Chatchai Sasakul in Bangkok, Thailand. Sasakul was the World Boxing

Council (WBC) **flyweight** champion. If Manny could win, he would be the world champion!

Most people thought Sasakul would win the match in his home country. It was just the second time that Manny had fought outside of the Philippines. Manny and Sasakul traded jabs and hooks. The crowd came alive when Sasakul landed a punch on Manny. But as the match wore on, Manny noticed Sasakul begin to tire. The champion breathed heavily. In the eighth round, Manny landed a big left-handed punch. Sasakul fell to the canvas. He tried to get up, but he fell again. The match was done. Manny was the new flyweight champion!

Manny married his wife, Jinkee, in 2000. They have five children: Emmanuel Jr., Mary Divine Grace, Israel, Queen Elizabeth, and Michael.

R2003659808

Manny celebrates a victory.

The victory made Manny a huge star in the Philippines. Suddenly everyone knew the name of the young man from Mindanao. In 2001, he won the International Boxing Federation (IBF) **super bantamweight** championship. Manny had won two world titles. But his biggest fights were still to come.

Marco Antonio Barrera shows energy and power in the ring.

COLLECTING TITLES

In 2003, boxer Marco Antonio Barrera had a record of 57 wins and just three losses. Manny faced Barrera on November 15 for the *Ring* magazine **featherweight** world title. Barrera was known for his strength and toughness. But he couldn't keep up with Manny's shocking speed.

Manny ducked and punched. He danced away and stepped in for powerful combinations. He knocked Barrera down in the third round. By round 11, it was clear Manny was going to win. Barrera's **corner team** threw in the towel. In boxing, throwing a towel into the ring is the corner team's way of saying they are ending the fight and acknowledging the opposing fighter as the winner.

Manny delivers a right hook to Barrera.

Manny punches Barrera in the nose.

"I'm surprised he lasted that long," Manny said later. The win marked Manny's third world title.

Manny wanted to help people in his home country. In 2007, he ran for a seat in the **House of Representatives** in the Philippines. But Manny didn't work hard to win the election. He had hoped that his popularity would be enough. Manny received less than half the votes and lost.

Manny ran for Congress in 2007.

Over the next few years, Manny moved in and out of different weight classes. Weight classes divide boxers by how much they weigh. Boxers fight only those boxers in their own weight class. Manny also kept taking on new fighters. In 2008, he won world titles against Juan

Manny loves basketball. He owns a basketball team in the Philippines. He even played in the Philippine Basketball Association.

Manuel Marquez and David Diaz. He also fought Oscar "The Golden Boy" De La Hoya that year. At 147 pounds, the boxing superstar was Manny's biggest foe yet. But Manny was too fast and strong for the Golden Boy. De La Hoya's eye was swollen shut by the eighth round. His corner team threw in the towel. It would be De La Hoya's last boxing match.

Manny carried the flag for the Philippines at the Opening Ceremony of the 2008 Olympic Games in Beijing, China.

In 2009, Manny beat Ricky Hatton for a world title. Then he took down Miguel Cotto for his second world championship of the year. The win against Cotto marked Manny's seventh career world title. He needed just one more in a new weight class to set the all-time record.

Manny waves to fans on the campaign trail in Manila, Philippines, two months before elections in 2010.

"A SPECIAL FIGHTER"

In 2010, Manny again ran for a seat in the House of Representatives. "This time, I am better prepared," he said. He won by about 60,000 votes. Manny had become a congressman!

Manny's next boxing challenge came in November. He fought Antonio Margarito for the **super welterweight** world title. Manny had already won seven world championships in seven weight classes. If he could beat Margarito, Manny would set a record with eight titles. About 50,000 fans stormed into Cowboys Stadium in Dallas, Texas, to see the fight.

Manny received the Congressional Medal of Distinction at the House of Representatives in Quezon City on November 22, 2010.

Manny *(left)* fights against Antonio Margarito *(right)*.

Margarito was five inches taller than Manny. The super welterweight champion's **reach** was six inches longer. He weighed 17 pounds more than Manny. Margarito was known for his hard punches and tough style. Some people thought Manny had finally chosen an opponent who was too big and tough.

Manny was all over Margarito from the beginning. Manny punched and ducked faster than his opponent could follow. In the fourth round, Manny smacked Margarito with a huge uppercut. The punch broke a bone in Margarito's face. His right eye swelled shut. But the big man fought on.

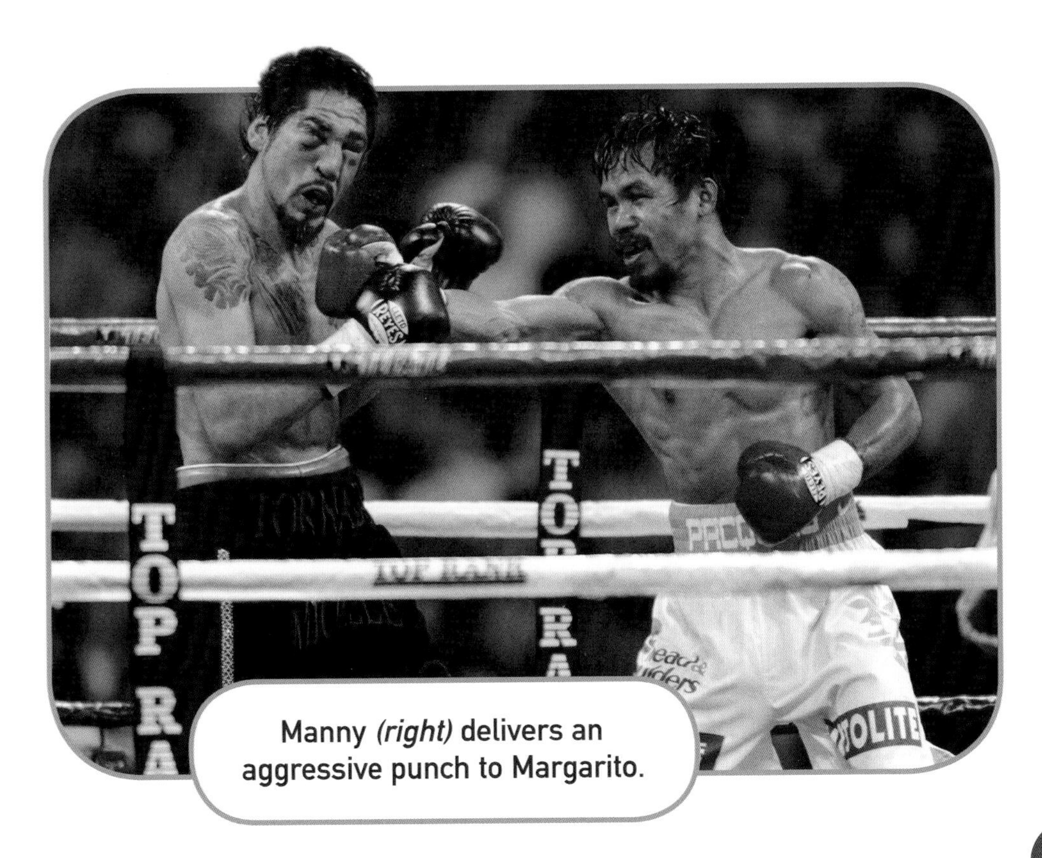

Manny *(right)* delivers an aggressive punch to Margarito.

Manny *(left)* and Antonio Margarito *(right)* hold up the super welterweight championship belt.

By the end of the fight, Margarito looked bloody and bruised. Manny looked tired but happy. The judges all agreed that Manny had won the fight. "I can't believe I beat someone that strong and big," Manny said. Margarito said Manny was "a special fighter."

Winning eight world titles in eight weight classes made Manny a boxing champion like no other. Over the next few years, people kept asking Manny about Floyd Mayweather. Mayweather had never been beaten. Boxing fans wanted to see if Manny could take him down.

Manny's best friend is a Jack Russell terrier named Pacman. The dog runs with Manny to help the boxer get ready for fights.

Mayweather *(left)* exchanges punches with Manny *(right)*.

After years of talk, Manny and Mayweather met in 2015. The match didn't end as Manny had hoped. But the event was still a success for both fighters. They each earned more than $100 million for one night of work!

Manny doesn't get too upset about losses in the ring. "It's just a game," he said. "Sometimes you win, sometimes you lose." As a boxer and a congressman, Manny wins more often than he loses.

Mayweather hugs Manny after defeating him in the May 2015 fight.

Selected Career Highlights

2015 Lost to Floyd Mayweather in the fight of the century

2010 Elected to the Philippines House of Representatives
Won eighth world title in a new weight class against Antonio Margarito

2009 Won seventh world title in a new weight class against Miguel Cotto
Won sixth world title in a new weight class against Ricky Hatton

2008 Defeated boxing superstar Oscar De La Hoya in eight rounds
Won fifth world title in a new weight class against David Diaz
Won fourth world title in a new weight class against Juan Manuel Marquez

2007 Lost election for Philippines House of Representatives

2003 Won third world title in a new weight class against Marco Antonio Barrera

2001 Won second world title in a new weight class against Lehlo Ledwaba

1998 Won first world title against Chatchai Sasakul

Glossary

bouts: boxing matches

combinations: fast series of punches

corner team: people such as trainers and doctors who help a boxer during a match

featherweight: a boxing weight class that usually goes up to 126 pounds

flyweight: a boxing weight class that usually goes up to 112 pounds

hooks: punches that come from the side of the body

House of Representatives: one of the groups of elected officials that makes laws in the Philippines

jabs: short, straight punches

martial arts: various sports that started as a means of self-defense

reach: the distance a fighter's arm can stretch

super bantamweight: a boxing weight class that usually goes up to 122 pounds

super welterweight: a boxing weight class that usually goes up to 154 pounds

trainer: a boxing coach

uppercut: a punch that goes up

Further Reading & Websites

Schraff, Anne. *Philippines*. Minneapolis: Lerner Publications, 2009.

Wells, Garrison. *Mixed Martial Arts: Ultimate Fighting Combinations*. Minneapolis: Lerner Publications, 2012.

The Official Manny Pacquiao Website
http://mp8.ph
Visit Manny's official website for news, gear, and much more about one of the world's most popular athletes.

PBS Kids—Solo Sports: Boxing
http://pbskids.org/itsmylife/body/solosports/article3.html
Read all about the sport of boxing including the gear, the history of the sport, and more.

Sports Illustrated Kids
http://www.sikids.com
The *Sports Illustrated Kids* website covers all sports, including boxing.

Expand learning beyond the printed book. Download free, complementary educational resources for this book from our website, www.lerneresource.com.

Index

Photo Acknowledgments

The images in this book are used with the permission of: © JOHN GURZINSKI/AFP/Getty Images, pp. 4, 7, 27, 28, 29; © Al Bello/Getty Images, p. 5; © Dondi Tawatao/Getty Images, p. 6; © Jason Merritt/Getty Images, p. 8; © Gerhard Joren/LightRocket/Getty Images, pp. 9, 11, 13; © Stanley Bielecki Movie Collection/Getty Images, p. 10; AP Photo/Sakchai Lalit, p. 14; © Jed Jacobsohn/Allsport/Getty Images, p. 16; © Jed Jacobsohn/Getty Images, p. 17; Reuters/Joe Mitchell/Newscom, pp. 18, 19; © ROBYN BECK/AFP/Getty Images, p. 20; AP Photo/Aaron Favila, p. 22; © NOEL CELIS/AFP/Getty Images, p. 23; Naoki Fukuda/AFLO/Newscom, pp. 24, 25; Gene Blevins/ZUMAPRESS.com/Newscom, p. 26.

Front cover: © Xaume Olleros/AFP/Getty Images.

Main body text set in Caecilia LT Std 55 Roman 16/28.
Typeface provided by Adobe Systems.